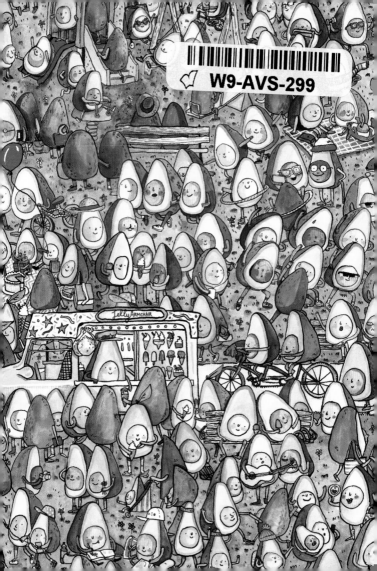

YOU'VE GUAC TO BE JOKING! I LOVE AVOCADOS!

Andrews McMeel
PUBLISHING®

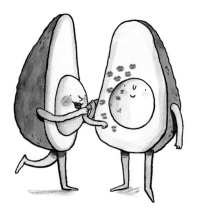

For Johno, Liz, Dad and Mum,
thanks for the puns and for
putting up with them.

PREHASSTORIC
DINEHASSAURS

TYRANNOSAURHASS

AVOCADODO

STONE HENGE

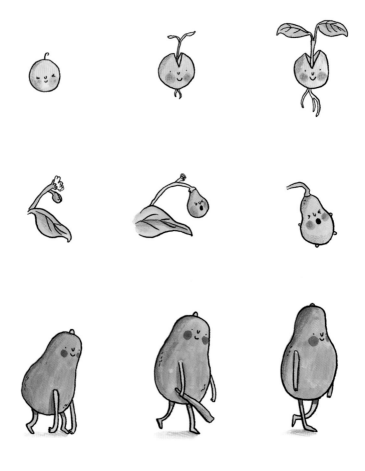

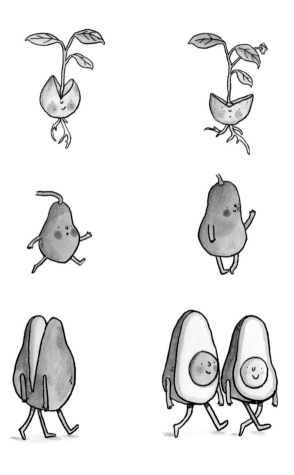

AVOLUTION

AVOCADO TOAST

SMASHED AVOCADO

AVOCATDO

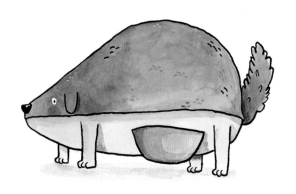

AVOCADOG

The WIZARD
AVOz

Harry pitter

and the
Hass-Blood Prince

VINCENT VAN GUAC

PABLO PICAVO

GRIZZLY PEAR

HASSTEA RETREAT

THE HAPPY PEAR

AVOCUDDLE

DOLLY PITON

HUGH GUACMAN IN

EGGS-MEN

THOMHASS EDISON

HOVERCADO

ORCHESTRA PITS

NOAH'S AVOARKDO

AVOCADUCKS

AVOCADO RAP

GUACAMOLE

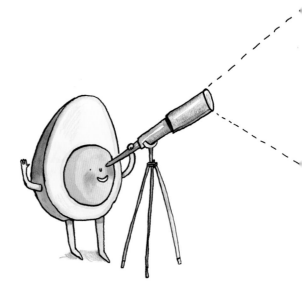

HASSTRONOMY

HASSTRONAUT

AVOCARPOOL

EMMA STONE

BRAD PIT

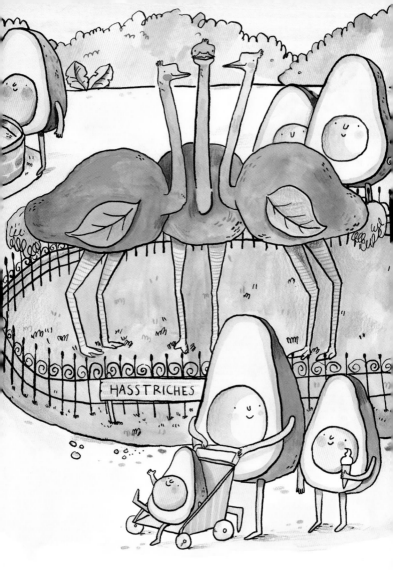

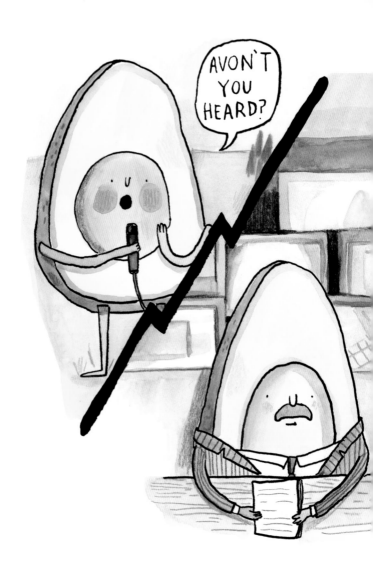

CRUSHED AVOCADO

THE LOVE GUACTOR

AVOTHA CHRISTIE

AVORIL LAVIGNE   PITNEY SPEARS

AVOCADO GRANDE

AVOCOWDO

PIT BULL

the CADO
on the RYE

ROLLING STONES

DAVID HASSELHOFF

AVOCADO DIP

AVOCARPDO

AVOSHARKDO

STATUE OF LIBPITY

THE GUAC WALL OF CHINA

STONE COLD STEVE AUSTIN VS THE GUAC

I SEE YOU
BABY

SHAKING
THAT HASS

SHAKING
THAT HASS

SHAKING
THAT HASS

RIPE HERE, RIPE NOW, RIPE HERE
RIPE NOW, RIPE HERE, RIPE NOW
RIPE HERE, RIPE NOW, RIPE HERE
RIPE NOW, RIPE HERE, RIPE NOW
RIPE HERE, RIPE NOW, RIPE HERE
RIPE NOW, RIPE HERE, RIPE NOW
RIPE HERE OW, RIPE HERE
RIPE NO RE, RIPE NOW
RIPE H , RIPE HERE
RIPE N , RIPE NOW
RIPE HE RIPE HERE
RIPE NO IPE NOW
RIPE HER PE HERE
RIPE NOW, RE, RIPE NOW
RIPE HERE, OW, RIPE HERE

THE BRAVOCADO

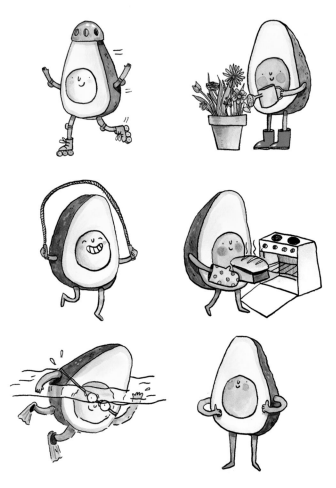

AVOCANDOS

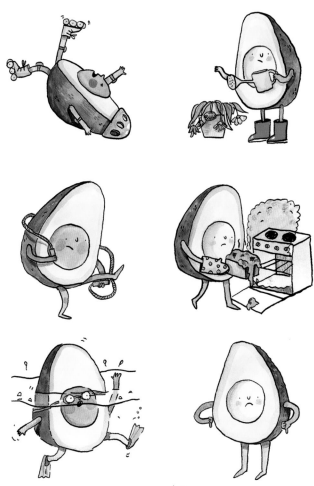

AVOCAN'T DOS

Guacula

Frankhasstein

HASS YOU LIKE IT

William Shakespeare

The Pit of

Dorian Green

BRUCE SPRINGSGREEN

AVOCARDGAME

FIFTY SHADES
OFGREEN

PITTY WOMAN

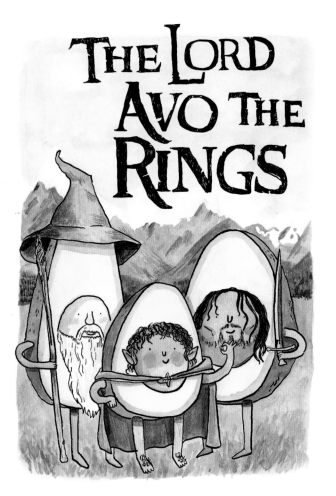

GAME of STONES

HE MAY BE SMALL & GREEN
BUT HE DOES AVOCADO

AVORAGE

AVOCADO ON
SOUR DOE

BUTCH HASSIDY
AND THE
SUNDANCE PIT

GUAC
HASSPECTATIONS

FRIDA KHAVO

AVO WARHOL

HASSASSINS

DIAMONDS ARE FORAVO

BAD HASS

HASSTA LA VISTA
BABY

HOLY GUACAMOLE

DEVIL'S AVOCADO

THE GREEN MILE

AVOTAR

BRIDGET STONES'S DIARY

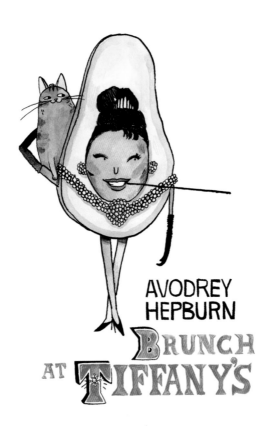

AVODREY
HEPBURN

Brunch AT Tiffany's

Louis Pitton   Guacci

GUAC MARTENS   AVOCARGO
                PANTS

MOUNT AVOREST

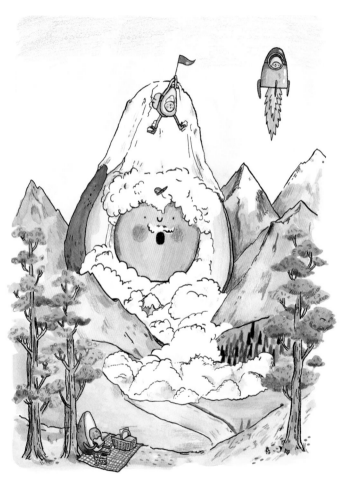

AVOLUNCH... AVOLANCHE... AVOLAUNCH

SEGREENA & VENHASS
WILLIAMS

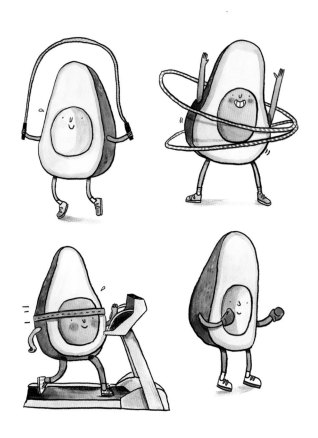

AVOCARDIO

THE OLYMPITS

THE BIG DIPPER

JUPITER

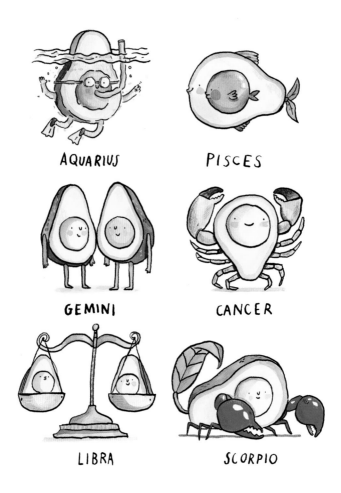

AQUARIUS

PISCES

GEMINI

CANCER

LIBRA

SCORPIO

HASSTROLOGY

ARIES

TAURUS

LEO

VIRGO

SAGITTARIUS

CAPRICORN

COLHASSEUM

THE ODHASSEY

AMERICAN RIPEO

CHILDREN
OF THE
AVOLUTION

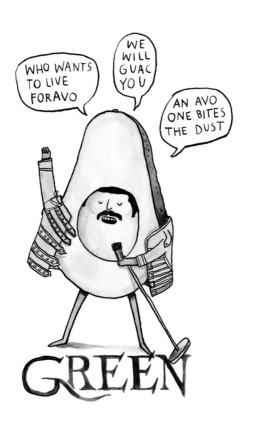

GuacAmore

Andrews McMeel Publishing
a division of Andrews McMeel Universal
1130 Walnut Street,
Kansas City, Missouri 64106

www.andrewsmcmeel.com
www.jellyarmchair.com

First published in 2019 by Pop Press,
an imprint of Ebury Publishing,
20 Vauxhall Bridge Road,
London SW1V 2SA

19 20 21 22 23 SDB 10 9 8 7 6 5 4 3 2 1

ISBN: 978-1-4494-9468-1

Library of Congress Control
Number: 2018955099

Editor: Jean Z. Lucas
Designer: Emily Voller
Art Director: Spencer Williams
Production Manager: Tamara Haus
Production Editor: Margaret Daniels

ATTENTION: SCHOOLS AND BUSINESSES

Andrews McMeel books are available at quantity discounts with bulk purchase
for educational, business, or sales promotional use. For information, please
e-mail the Andrews McMeel Publishing Special Sales Department:
specialsales@amuniversal.com.